T0105514

FROM GRASS TO *GRACE*
From Rags to Riches

Dapo ademola Omisore

FROM GRASS TO GRACE
From Rags to Riches

iUniverse books may be ordered through booksellers or by contacting:

iUniverse
1663 Liberty Drive
Bloomington, IN 47403
www.iuniverse.com
1-800-Authors (1-800-288-4677)

ISBN: 978-1-4620-0704-2 (sc)
ISBN: 978-1-4620-0705-9 (e)

Print information available on the last page.

iUniverse rev. date: 01/25/2016

THE INVISIBLE AND IMPERCEPTIBLE HAND

Scores of events transpired mysteriously. Chains of occurrences happened most amazingly. Legions of issues rear their ugly heads most astonishingly – logical answers elude us. Events that can only be praised regardless and irrespective of their nature and magnitude still needs to be explained.

The assurance of the presence of God notwithstanding I was quite frankly and in all honesty besieged with loneliness unhappiness, sadness and dejection I can no longer withstand.

Keeping in mind all these experiences took place in the confinement and comfort of the four walls of the church some folks outside probably do not experienced these phenomenal troubles even though they are largely unchurched.

I should have been solaced and glad essentially, my presence in the church should have invoke and provoke in me some form of gratification.

I should have been cherished. In a split second so much had happened so quickly, in a fraction of a minute my greatest fear quietly, discreetly, and momentarily surfaced.

It seemed everything had compounded and I was about to lodge a complaint I was rapidly on the verge and brink of succumbing.

From nowhere out of the blue surrounded by an array of people I felt the figurative touch of a hand. The grip was fleeting but vehement and firm.

Eventually at the end of his brief and memorable encounter. I was highly impressed and understand.

I cast my gaze around wondering, puzzled and perturbed I was slightly disturbed painstakingly I glanced again has anyone touched me by chance I imagined there was no one in sight the unseen hand touch is geared towards the enhancement, enrichment and perfection of my reliance, conviction and confidence in God. He is too reliable to disown his own. All weakness, feebleness and frailness received appreciable and considerable strength I was consequently reinvigorated, revitalized and spiritually strengthened.

Multi-Faceted Face of Color

The rainbow is an exact replica of the multiplicity of color. Joseph's coat is duplication of the multi-functioning and usefulness of color.

Look at a jewel in an encrusted case.

Better still, consider the skin of the whole human race.

Take a moment to examine the trees, the flowers, and the birds.

A feeling of awe and a sense of wonder is birthed.

Panoramas of color, delightful to see.

In unconditional and unfathomable love he created them all. But man has altered and marred the colors by way of sin. This singular act on the part of man culminated into disgrace.

The color of greed predominates, the color of pure and undiluted love is redundant.

All colors must as a necessity truly blend when we come to the end, when all humanity stand face to face before the judgment seat of the most sagacious judge of all time (Jesus Christ).

Where Do You Really Fit-In

Where do you fit-in in his plan
The one who created all things both in Heaven
And here on earth Below
Indeed he is a master planner
who had Creatively Create
And artfully and ingeniously made
Everything without using any indigenious materials
There is room for everyone
He is a God that accomodates
His Primary Purpose is to accelerates Anyone.
Who will exhibit an infinitesimal Amount
Of Humility since he is infinite.
Humility as small as mustard seed
He entertains and welcome
And in no wise or circumstance Rejects
For he never reckons with circumference
As this play no role in the day of reckoning
When all acts and deeds is giving recognition
With him mankind must reconcile
Thankfully he made a provision
No consternation is necessary

The Progression of the New Period

With civilization, modernization, advancement and technology there are a brisk and swift waves of teeming exposure to tremendous development. Which in turns brings a clear-cut improvement with explosion of knowledge, jet-like lives on the run, new thoughts on religion, new governing ways economy, crime, the decadent displays, opiates of peace promised soon in our time and days.

The world can testify and vouch for seeing a galaxy of these things previously. This is not a matter of presumption, truly and realistically they have seen it before however the time of increase are in full gear, swing and force and each of his follies and maladies the world hastily and hurriedly will endorse. The days of the locust must indisputably and incontestably run their full course what that age-old serpent damage and destroys

More Grease to Your Elbow

Each of us has different calling, it is your sole responsibility to decipher and decide the divine call.

Hesitantly and hastily seek the counsel of the savior who will readily and unreluctantly divulge and disclose your earthly mission and his divine master-plan.

Irrespective and irregardless of our station in life, whatever that may be regardless of what we eventually become, each of us has a primary and principal role to play and a purpose to accomplish to help alleviates and ameliorates the burdens of some. Offering assistance and helping hands to the widows and orphans is welcome. Unresponsive to the their plights and plea to say the least is most unwelcome. Helping this category and class of people is good giving aid to the hungry and cold multitudes are homeless, jobless, helpless while manifold number of people are lonely and old. Keep the good work. Do not rest on your oars. Keep the flag flying and working your utmost best at all times and in all situations pleases the father and son quickly and swiftly a star is added to your crown and is laced there by him – a reward for a job well done.

Wrecked

Many life have been wrecked. Multiple of souls have been ruined. Life that are destined for success, through human lack of sanctity and sacredness for life, become largely and totally walloped.

So innocent and pure, it's little soul secure. Created by almighty God, destroyed by man. Rob of any opportunity to live, granted no chance to give.

Repose Trust In Me My Child

Child, where is your trust, the one you previously possessed. You are presently deviating and more and more becoming increasingly defiant to all my entreaties and "pleads". Are you now insinuating that I am no longer trustworthy.

My word audibly and audaciously speaks loud and clear – behold child the end and close of this age is dangerously drawing near. I and I only your (creator) knows the exact, precise day, time and hour and without mincing word child, believe me I am clearly in control and power. The entire creation was my handiwork, I created the universe, I made you all dear child, dearly and indisputably passionately I loved you, but you purposely proposed to build a demacation wall between thee and me. You have strayed, swayed and turned away. Needless and suffice to say I no longer hear when last did you pray, when last did you repose and release faith when last in words, thoughts, deeds and actions exhibited thou child, faithfulness in me second after second, minute after minute hour after hour you pitch you tent with the scoffers constantly and continuously reject all my utterances and all I had done.

Plus the reason and rationale behind the sacrificial love of my only son believe me child, it is already late there is no more room for tarrying, I simply and frankly cannot wait every soul must sooner than later, incontestably and irrefutably give full account of thoughts and deeds in life's recount.

My son is a sagacious judge, he is fair and has a flair for truth. Patiently, he has been waiting for this while for you tell me here and now what your response to him "I disbelieved. You were, simply put, nothing short of a whim. Oh my dear child, I beseech you. This day as always to desist from acting foolishly.

Do not be numbered with those that perilously and persistently sinned and shunned me. they are fool-hardy

Stop sealing your fate, wholeheartedly accept my beloved son, this is a time-sensitive matter, and it does not lend itself to debate. My word is both sure and settled, I will soon appear. My beloved child, believe me, the time is here.

The Antidote

Overwhelmed, overburdened and overcome by oppressions?
Dismayed, disillusioned and disenchanted by depressions?
Preoccupied, possessed and pursued by possessions?
<u>Cure all by mere confessions</u>.

Emptiness

Vague and void is a life without Christ.
Vile and volite is a life devoid of grace
All he does unquestionably ends in unimaginable chaos since he is christless and not Christ-like.
He stands the risk of strings and streams of crisis.
An empty life exacts it's cost of meaning that is forever lost, so beloved brothers and sister in Christ lift up those eyes to greet the sun, move those feet slowly but steadily, swiftly and sincerely, steadfastly and systematically to make them run effectively and efficiently. Use those hands till day is done to string those precious, palatable and very paramount pearls you left unstrung.

Categorization

With all due consideration, categorize yourself.
Where do you belong.
Beloved of God, are all your belongings.
Here or hereafter.
Are you preparing or daily engaging in frivolity and fickleness.

Are you ensuring with the passage of each day, your body wholly and whole-heartedly presented to the one who rightly must have you in possession. Which one are you in actuality are you truly gold or hay, do not jump into conclusion in haste. There is still ample time and opportunity for activation.

Remember brothers and sisters in Christ, we are not made with a spirit of fear, we are to seek strength and succor from him, put, discard and shelve aside all manners of doubts, to walk courageously and circumspectly in his light not ignoring all possible flight. The prophetic pronouncement of the latter times are being fulfilled before our very eyes, in our present day, our pathway to Christ and cross, has been permanently and perpetually settled and paid in full, the choice is entirely yours', you can peradventure and possibly arrive there as gold or stubble and hay?

Multiple Directions

There are multiplicity of roads. What I am quite desirous of is not the load.

There are several roads I may have attempted.

Where they could have led I certainly cannot ascertained.

I neither care nor am I keenly interested in all these godforsaken roads.

They offer nothing else other than foreboding reminiscences.

Consequent upon his grace, the road I eventually tried, trod and tirelessly embarked on proved to awakened me from my spiritual slumber rather profusely. A firmer faith and trust emanated, as this road becomes more and more clear, the end result of this experience was significantly typical.

Distinctly it showed how he will safe-guard me.

From the dreadful darkness of the night roads.

From potentially disturbing and frightening starkness of my lost ways.

How he will constantly and continuously share his sublime light to direct and navigates the rough terrain of darkness.

In bright tomorrows not dark yesterdays my Lord and master Jesus Christ sovereignly ?????????

Pledges

The entire universe is littered with antichrists.

Their patron is yet to surface, he is on his way.

Side by side with his devotees and cohorts and emissaries, along with the legion of his poltergeists.

His primary mission is to lure and lead astray.

Weak-minded beings, so gullible in every sense of the word.

Vain-seekers, seeking for that which is not lost.

Dogmatically Believing anything and everything.

Easily out maneuvered, out-paced, and outwitted through sugar-coated words believing what we will the promises that only feign to sate us and fulfil.

There is a supreme-being (God) whose word is tested, and proven to be true by all standards and accounts.

His words is comprehensive.

His words is complete.

His words is tried.

His word is triumphant.

His promises was fore known.

His ways was foreordained.

A promise of life abundant awaits those who search for him dutifully.

Those who spare nothing but wholeheartedly seek for him diligently.

This promise was reserved, preserved for the few.

Of those who ceaselessly, constantly and continuously seek this throne.

His infinitely strong hand upholds, his tenacious and firm grip is a stronghold for all and sundry who will follow his directives and directions.

This pledge was for those through thick and thin serve him faithfully.

This promise is restricted it has some form of restraint you must throughout your entire lifetime create time out of no time for fellowshipping. His angels readily and regularly sing with joy.

And by his strength those few withstand all onsets and assaults to destroy.

Leaning

The end of the scheme of earthly things is approaching the close of age of this maddened word is accelerating. Time no longer can transcend the ages that have uselessly, unproductively and unbeneficially whirled.

With stupendous, sustaining lightning with unimaginable, unstoppable frightening speed.

To end in this abyss we are all living witnesses of all that have been decreed.

We have reached the precipe.

Two options exist

Stopping or moving ahead better still, variety of devices we are envisaging to spearhead or now charlantly rushing ahead? Angels fear to tread the very ground our wicked ways have led. We are indisputably at a crossroad suffice and needless to say we are at brink and verge of indecision now is the appropriate time to decide the way we want to ?? the narrow path? or the broad or the wide road. The ball is in our court. Courting one means neglecting the other. Where will you look to know?

The Multi-Faceted Faces of Sounds

There are multiplicity of sounds, the sound of this world all make their ascent unto heaven, where they represent the posthumous of time and mankind's descent.

Into a solemn an awful lament. Unholy curses, the bedrock of fights. The contention and agitation such outcry incites. Violent and vehement affliction of malaise and blight.

Sounds of a bigot wrapped up in feigned and fake pride. Sounds of the enthusiasts with cries that misguide.

Sounds of each war with starvation astride.

The sounds of mankind in blunt and stark genocide.

In your sound of withering and putrification. In your sound of decay, in your sound of decomposition be quiet! Be still!

Your deafening and blaring noise was not meant to fill my universe, and I have heard you until my patience is thin. Only I and I only can fulfil.

The blessed and prosperous life you covet and crave for now hear be, behold me, be attentive and embrace my vow, such sounds in your generation I will disallow.

Some will be reaping while others yet plow. Scores of people are uncaring, legions of people bluntly refuse to hear, seemingly scared, they prefer to live in their fear.

It's this world they cherish, relish; this world they revere.

Their struggle and scuffle was littered with profanity they howl for more gain.

Their sounds constantly profane such debacles of sin just to obtain in hardness and deafness they will remain. Those who have leaning and inclination toward wisdom hesitate not to seek my counsel in prayer. The current sounds heralds and prepare for it is a fore runner of the fast approaching time when all is put to rest and laid bare. The sound of my voice (Almighty God's voice) will terminates this affair.

The sheep and the goats must necessarily and compulsorily part ways.

The present sounds in this universe are mere caricature, resemblance and display of our feelings toward the loving-God, our only valid and authentic resumes to finite joys or eternal dismays.

The Clarion

A fascinating, electrifying and astonishing time is around the corner and it lies just up ahead a time that clearly defies description.

A time of indescribable and tremendous joy or a time of unimaginable deep dread.

A time of sundown or sunrise.

A trumpet's extremely audible sound signaling the end of this earthly affairs are compelling and vivid feature my Lord (Jesus Christ) rightly advised to watch for.

Those of us who are rapturable will join him in the clouds of sky,

Perpetually and everlastingly to know and be known.

Christ likeness will be rewarded, wickedness will receive it's fair share of punitive measure.

There is more yet for heaven and earth, assuring salvation, stealing the fate of the elects, the commencement of the judging of each soul's rebirth.

Only a fool hardy individual in his pride can defiantly challenge and foolishly deny the undiluted truth that has always been told. Just hearing for hearing sake and men apparently frivolously edifies the secular things they behold.

The righteous minded will hear and joyfully, cheerfully and jubilantly accept Jesus as their savior and Lord. Via the avenue of faith and unswervering, unwavering and persevering trust. They everlastingly and eternally kept their vibrant hope for a greater compensation and reward.

In a fraction of a second, faster by all standards and accounts than the speed of light.

We will all answer the call to meet him, some souls will undoubtedly surrender, while some multitudes will vehemently fight, how many are willing, ready and fully prepared to be there to exchange pleasantries with him?

Belated

There is an individual so deaf, nor anyone so blind.

Obstinately refusing to hear, unwilling to see.

God's purpose and plan for his destiny.

His mind-set is unbending, unyielding and he loathes and detest trying. He hates discussion and dislike ratification of the deep things of soul, the meaning of life; He has completely forgotten that his future commences in after-life.

He continuously and constantly stumbles and grope in darkness, feeling his way, unable to decipher and fathom day after day the missing items in the equation and scheme of things.

He miserably and colossally lacks the hope that only faith brings.

Somewhere, someday, sometime he will realize his monumental loss, he will yearn and long for the one who died on the cross his stiffneckedness-deviance authenticates the sorrowful fact that he just waited too post-humously (belatedly).

The Travesty of the Ultimate Robbers

A package of lesson exist for a willing and learning heart.

A lesson the Holy Bible unearthed about Judas the ultimate thief who robbed his own soul of his eternal belief.

He traded the heavenly pleasure for earthly possession.

Satan pitched the debacle of sin of betrayal and denial at his doorstep.

All his concentration and focus was on the inherent gain.

The grand theft of the ages but he colossally failed in vain.

His silver became too tainted, it was rather too hot to handle it was too heavy to hold and behold. His conscience became tanished and seared because his master was sold.

Covetousness and greed gained upper hand in chagrin.

He could not continue with the devilish thoughts held within.

Esau was another character meriting mentioning who traded and exchanged his birthright for a mere meal. He sold his inheritance for trifling and momentary respite.

Ananias, insidious and vile, was another thief worthy of note. He stole from his maker, God, to pocket unending grief.

Are you a traitor? Drawn and tempted by worldly possessions.

Torn-apart by the love of the world vis-a-vis the love for your savior you are now in the valley of indecision. Are you currently planning to sell your Lord (Jesus Christ) for earthly residue. Declining his entreaties is an emblem of robbery. You dare not rob him of his due. And our theft is the same as theirs in his view.

Popularity

Fortunes and fame, material things believe it or not some folks lack neither of the two in abundance, in enormity they have these twins.

They have it all seasons of sun with sustained magic that brings the entire world at their call.

It seems their body is age-proof they live on forever young always vibrantly healthy and strong sparkling like gems, they became celebrities - household names whose praises are sung.

And they can do no wrong. They are exempted from any harm and havoc the considered forgotten bunch who can merely have their lunch. The run of the mill the collection of dreamers still daydreaming for a place and portion in the sun, fervently hoping and scavenging and clamoring to fill our role as befitting survivors.

We experienced both aches and ailments. Clearly, vividly and unmistakably we show our age always bemoaning the fact that we are weak.

We try to cope but woefully fail to selfguage and completely oblivious of the fact that we too are unique.

God distributes a measure of talents to all and sundry even though by all accounts and estimation, all are not alike.

Some are remarkably and noticeably humble, while some are privileged to have status, and some could be aptly described as hidden light.

Most of the world consists of unknowns keeping in mind each one has a unique gift that part in ourselves no other individual or mortal being can lay claim to or owns our own special way and means to upliftment.

The Swing Box

Is time to you swing box swinging and sweeping your hands in readiness to mock swinging and dancing from side to side in preparation to crock Mr. Pendulum, swaying and swerving from one end to another each ticking sound a hollow knock. That brings about a callous shock.

Mr. Clock highlights and announces the day's task.

It says among other things there are an array of things to do and you should know.

You are relentless in your skill and speed and you will surely show that "someday soon" is much too slow.

A clock should remind us of things earmarked for a brand new day for your launching launching yourself into limelight. Willingly, cheerfully, happily helping as many as you possibly can providing selflessness and candidness to those less fortunate and less privileged than you.

You have the effrontery and the audacity to say, "My time is to be utilize and use for lovely and laudable ventures and undertaking, not to abuse it is not meant to be wasted, it is not to lose. The only one (God) who transcends time and all things seen and unseen, visible and invisible gives us time and life renews.

Golden and Flamboyant Lifestyle

Golden goose you have been out paced you have out ran, outwitted and out maneuvered.

Our demands outpaced your's for we have been playing fast and loose we have run with outstretched hands.

Our eyes increasingly grow bigger than our pocket and purse – consequently each time we look the things we see we absolutely want we will get them now by hook or crook and cost just does not count.

Strings of goodies to select from a peck of things to do mortal beings by nature wants it all, the maximum, the fullest, the optimum eat our cake and still retain it has been our slogan refrain, we want to have our cake notwithstanding too.

From time-to-time big brother and big sister engages in lavish and wanton generosity and giveaways, we dutifully and dexterously stand in line for our fair share thinking that someday we woo will become a shareholder.

We are seduced in such a manner in an era and age of stupendous showers.

Wined, dined and danced, all these we have justifiably and unjustifiably executed the piper requests that will must pay now.

We have crushed and crashed that golden egg supply and therefore abruptly halts our holiday.

As the heavens differs in altitude and attitude to the earth so also are the things we need and the things we want.

They are poles apart in divergence.

They are noticeably two separate things.

The golden goose? Do no be fooled, there is no such breed.

Our incessant and enormous wants have clipped its wings.

Reaping

Where are honor and truth?

Where are the innocent youth?

Each paradigm brings a change and a shift in our times and ties unseen beginning and uncertain end.

Our collective and individual harvest is yielding and producing untended seeds.

?? cycles of selfishness, self-centeredness and unbridled deeds.

We, to our detriment decides to place self infinitely far ahead and above our God

Mind you, to be forewarned is to be forearmed.

The grapes of his wrath are now being trod.

At a glance, a cursory look reveals the results of our everyday shame. There is no necessity for anymore divine revelation.

In pious denouncements we pass and shift and heap the blame for miserable and manifold failures. We find too difficult to admit, court lawsuits will verify that we are certainly not unfit. Sins of our ancestors are no longer actent. They are surfacing now in our time and day presently – our children never ceases to show how godless and heartless the universe had become.

The gospel has answers for all and sundry who are willing, waiting, pressing and preparing to come.

Doors Opened

Recounting, recalling, re-examining recreating and rethinking all hurts, the tears and the heartaches of the yesteryears.

The sorrows and the pains of years gone by.

The anguish of being alone times and occasion when you anticipate your heart is about exploding or when you no longer consider more exploration when you envisage your entire body system will break.

recalling the sadness you have experienced and known.

Be rest assured your Lord cares. None of your tears escapes his keen, sage witty, omniscient eyes.

Be comforted, be encouraged, he had gently and soothingly wipe them away. Remember he is your solace, comfort and cavalier.

Do not you know he hears each time you say I am lonely and in desperate and dire need of direction.

He is not a dictator in any way or manner but a supreme and sovereign God who lovingly gives divine guidance and directives to those divinely called.

He takes your hand and providentially leads you to a deeper understanding of himself and teach you the advantages and benefits inherent and inbred in selflessness. Can you see how his unfeigned and unfathomable love opens new doors for you.

Inconsistent and Unplanned Lives

Those so aimless, thoughtless, nonchalant, carefree and careless those who takes their precious lives for granted.

Bluntly refused to shun anything but always admitted lives of vapor that are not prayerful and are restless, disenchanted.

All those who are tossed to and fro as the wind and those who trek the indecernible and indistinct ways where do their maze of adventure ends.

How can they accurately and aptly justify their days?

A galaxy of people who frankly speaking drift along unchallenged by the urgent need to learn that void and vacuous souls will only prolong the tenor, trend and trending of their concern. Unknowledgeable, unlearned, unwise and plainly vacant and void of God's design and plans for all their heedless lives to say the least are not deployed to accomplish, attain and achieve anything beyond their terribly thin wall.

Changeable Styles

Human history is replete with instability. Mankind, from generation to generation has an history shrouded in inconsistency.

Male and female created he them only those two spices or gender none other than these two.

But alternate styles knell a requiem.

by uttering – the word – we're another.

Genetic pitfalls are seldom indeed and true epicemes are few.

Alternative live by their self-styled creed professing and proclaiming themselves as new.

This fashion, format and structure is older than history.

There is practically nothing hidden about this at all.

A mere repetition of the same story of man pre-emptying God's call.

The sin is repugnant and repulsive, a mockery contrary to God's own will. A direct product of man's debauchery a shining and striking example of his consistent slide downhill.

Trespassers and transgressors can most certainly turn on a new leaf, they can change, they have the choice,

Which option and priority is first? Illicit and invalid lust? A golden chance and criteria to rejoice in an undiluted, unprecedented and unfeigned love accursed?

Our Labor

Our labor, our sweat the sum total of our skill and speed.

Sweet memories of days of sweltering.

Another day, another dollar. Initially we scream, thereafter we shiver that we cannot make it stretch to it's optimal and maximal capacity.

Our daily bread now costs a fortune, a bundle.

Each new day, brings new toil, it is off we trundle.

Every blesseth day poses new dexterity and each dexterity a trail of new devil back to work to stop and fetch.

We consider our job an open pits, we presume and perceive it grinds us piece by piece, bit by bit, needless to say we worth a whopping raise and we deserve to be praised. The boss-man overlook, our request is overturned to say the least, the boss-man is cold and the whole thing is dumb. Mind you we are the star for we are their plum.

The whole idea is inflated our ego is crushed, consequently we bluntly refuse to submit perhaps we are clearly out of sync it is crystal clear the world is rough and certainly enough a lot of walls we hit are tremendously tough.

This is a product of our pattern of thinking.

Disengaging From Active Duty

Thank God I can quit I can safely retire.

The grisly grind is perpetually over.

I can sit back, relax all day long and simply admire my new-found field of clover.

I cast my mind back on my sweat and labor.

Casting a light of reflection on the work I have done they merit remembrance those times of toil and times I groan the innumerable steps and miles I have run are all reminiscences of the times I certainly could call my own.

I can both joyfully and gleefully deactivate. That is proudly and absolutely what I do. There is no legal operandi to tolerate the gulf of work. Goodbye, adieu.

Initially I thought I had finally escaped the task-master task and then it dawned on me and hit I must be getting old.

The last thing I want to settle for is to rock and knit.

Quite frankly I am appalled for not being told.

I cannot sit back wearing and wanting I should not spend my remaining years diminishing and deteriorating.

God forbid laying and twiddling thumbs making provision for something inside longing and yearning for wanting out of need. To be needed becomes a summons that constantly and continuously stirs me about.

God of heaven and earth, may thy will permits these fragile and delicate bones to move around. In all sincerity, retirement from active service is indeed profound.

My humble submission and conclusion is retiring from life is for twits.

Aphorism (Reflection)

Words of reflection not words of refraction moments of progression not periods of retrogression are our expectations and anticipation.

We mortal being complains and we are always complacent by so doing our problems compounds. And we end up not having companion.

We all gripe and all grumble each time life throws a tumble do not be bitter when you stumble each crash-course is meant to humble.

Embrace and acknowledge your lots and utter a prayer.

You ought not to rant and swear you should be rest assured satan does not actually care.

How extremely and extraordinarily hard you fall for your welfare.

If no one else cares Jesus does and he certainly and constantly hears every word. He knows exactly what is transpiring be warned and be careful that you have not slurred.

His precious and prestigious name in vain when sprawl occurred.

Those many bumps typifies and amplifies and tears apart or fortify each uttered word will testify how you demean, destroy and deteriorate or glorify.

Subterfuge (Untruth)

Uneasy lies the head that wears a crown uneasy lies the mouth that lie.

As it stands the risk of being decrowned.

Untruth no matter how discreetly and decently packaged contains no pact.

though it possesses unproductive and unprofitable powerless power in actuality it is not powerful as it is not impactful but tactful and artful.

The innumerable excuses we forment and fabricate each day.

The uncountable white fibs that flows forth from our lips.

The things we concur and concludes as the truth slips away.

Are sometime subtle, deceptive and smoothly equips.

The venture into more virulunt lies these may cause havoc, harm, appall or destroy they weave the web of our willful demise the liar consequently and continuously becomes the devils envoy.

Our lies offers no help whatsoever beyond this world and life it is not gainful and graceful for afterlife.

Will our lies includes or excludes us from eternity with God.

Will it separates and segregates us from God

Will our lies be believed on judgment day?

Will heaven be outsmarted and outwitted and out maneuvered by what we say.

I say no way!

Each lie that we tell will only propel us deeper and deeper into our own self-made hell.

The Memorable Individual

The special individual makes his mark on the sound of time.

He leaves a legacy that transcends, that is transparent, and also transforms.

His acts and actions, deeds and demeanor, mannerism and maturity exceeds the expectations of his days and time. His influence upon his generation sparks and spearheaded, tenacity, faith and abiding trust.

We all ardently and fervently wish to do mighty things.

We all crave and cry for huge dreams.

To be the indelible and memorable hero we are constantly compelled to pull the strings, and be the synosure of all eyes and the center-stage star that gleans and gleams.

We have the intention and the intuition to save the whole world.

We like to sample and savor the zeniths of prudence and praise for being that special and spectacular someone who grandly hurled out goodness, greatness and lovely bouquets.

Then we abruptly came to a crashing conclusion and confronted and contest with stark and striking realities that we are just ordinary people doing and delving into the world of extraordinary.

And the bubblets burst and we must awake embrace and face the incontestible and indisputable fact that we are just plain everyday people who quiver and quack at any thought of discomfort, displeasure and pain.

In actuality a hero who is worthy of the word in every sense maximizes and optimizes every opportunity that is tossed his ways to help the helpless and provide a voice to the voiceless and also defend the cause of defenceless.

A real hero serves in quiet dignity giving his entirety and totality without any thought of reward or award to help those in need, to cater, to comfort and to free. A real hero serves the only real master and Lord.

Safe-Landing

Thank God, the raging sea of life does not consume.

Lift your hands in praise and your mouth in praiseology to the only – and only miraculous and mighty sailor for you have not been condemned.

Paddle your boat, firmly, fistfully pull that oar.

Accelerates and accentuates the gear and head for shore.

Row as tremendously and tenaciously hard as you have never rowed before.

Beckoning, bewildered and boisterous seas will call no more.

You have been adrift, you have been aground you are now in safe arms.

And certainly dismantle, destroy, disengage and disenable and disarm.

You have floated far, you have been around, suffice and needless to say, you have seen those ?? violent and mischievous waves that can surreptitiously and stealthily surround and nebulously and neatly swamp you in their roaring sound.

Your sea consist and comprise of beleaguered and brisk winds that tempts and lure and simply and frankly pretends.

To offer a great deal, but always ends in infinitely deeper depths of deluge than mind intends.

In sight is the safelanding, and is just ahead, you are water-logged and perceived and presumed half-dead, you perseveringly and prevailingly pray your boat will stay a-tread and you will safely reach your destination the watershed.

My Fantasy

My hankering, yearning and longing is to go backward through the years.

My first desire is to wipe my mother's tears.

I will ease her uncountable heartaches.

The hurts she cleverly endeavored to cover.

I will temper my impatience.

I will create time out of no time to embark on rediscovery.

The motive for her selflessness the reason responsible for indescribable love and earnestness.

All the painstaking sacrifices and dreams forfeited and ignored I am ready and prepare to honor. How I fervently and ardently wish I can unwind and rewind the clock, it is rather too late for such a cloak.

This only lies in the realm of wistfulness.

She already departed this world to the world beyond where there are no aches where there is no existence of heartaches.

Where there is no lack.

Where there is no room for levity.

There is conspicuous absence of bemoaning.

There is no legal standi for bewilderment.

I missed my chance. I cannot go back. My aspiration lies in the distance my ambition is dislodged.

Tempted Beyond Measure

I succumbed to temptation.

I committed costly and avoidable mistakes.

I harmed and injured innumerable souls.

I played for high stakes.

The insidious blush.

The illegitimate flush.

The illegal sensuousness.

The illicit sensation.

The demands and its takes.

I was no longer capable to handle and tackle the eventual sustained wounds that it makes.

My life was careening.

My world was awry.

The totality of my life was askew.

The damage was astounding.

The crash was astronomical.

I could still hopefully utilize the rubble and debris under-utilized. Gather together the pieces of my fragmented life.

Mend the damaged life.

Join together the disjointed life.

Connect together the disconnected life.

My life could commence anew.

I threw the past into the sea of oblivion.

All that transpired then I am oblivious of.

With eagerness and earnestness I look forward to a new dawn.

A life dotted and donned with grace.

My Soul

Oh, imposter of the devil, relentlessly you have waged war.

You have been unceasing in your unleashing of your onslaught and wallop.

You saw a feebleness.

Clearly there is a weakness.

Let me pitch my tent here.

I must stay perpetually and abode.

Abidingly Here not there.

You successfully, surreptitiously crept into my heart.

You engaged with me what you considered a heart to heart talk.

Wanting to take dominance.

Attempting to take dominance.

Attempting to take total and complete governance.

You tossed every imaginable pleasure my way.

You removed morality far away.

Goodness is unnecessary.

Morality is uncalled for.

Credibility is a sheer waste of time, suffice to say it is unwarranted, you said loosen up and we unlock those golden, memorable and unspeakable joys now in dry-dock.

Perseveringly, you commenced hunting and hurting. You have a vision and a mission.

Embarking on a lifetime of censuring. Tirelessly looking for every opportunity to engage in fault-finding unabatedly you nurture low esteem, dislike and disapprove all that are potentially flaw-less.

You granted the license to do anything and everything I deem fit.

Go ahead and be involved in act of atrocity. You promised mutual benefit. You ultimate plan is to take the soul, rip and split.

I danced to it's tune unwatchful, I strictly adhere to his advice. It turned out to be a ill-advice.

Alas, it was a misgiving in haste and waste I made by bed he had a sumptuous grip and mark on my soul. And consequently left me dead.

I heard a still, small and soft voice beckoning insistently whispering persistently my child, my precious child, to say the least, you have been headstrong. And the harms, havoc and damage you have done to yourself may be life-long.

I am your only hope.

All other ways and approaches are terribly hopeless.

Make me your true delight.

Be mindful of the caricature of satan for he is truly delirious.

Embrace faith.

Disregard and overlook sight.

I certainly and incontestably have the capability and the wherewithal necessary to lead you home through the night. The impostor had long departed. Myself and (Jesus Christ) will never ever again parted.

Summary and Conclusions

Clearly, we have just scratched the surface when it comes to understanding all of the stabilization needs of the candle industry.

Ciba is committed to investing the time and resources necessary to study and understand your needs by working with you to design stabilizer systems which reflect your particular needs, both today and in the future.

A Second Change

Rewinding the details of your past life.

Replaying the events of your disjointed past.

Piecing together the pieces of your fragmented life.

Granted the chance to relieve your life afresh. Are there things you will unambiguously do anew.

Are there changes you will like to consider. Are there any adjustments that merits your regard.

In a fresh start would you like to set in motion a switch of restart.

Purposing in your heart to release a wind of benevolence to the less-fortunates.

Prayerfully considering attending to the needs of the less-priviledged.

Thoughtfully selecting the right word to convey and earnestly utilizing every medium to assists and console.

Would you cheerfully give whenever the need arises.

When a demand is placed on your wallet, would you obstinately close your eyes and turn deaf ears to all entreaties. Would you swiftly and voluntarily entreat would you willingly give your time would you joyfully maximize the use of your talents?

Would you choose the pathway of hoarding, or opt for and pitch your camp with immeasurable and boundless hospitality?

Would you be thankful for the strings of blessings received?

Would you be grateful for the arrays of divine endowments collected?

Would you justifiably apportioned a space for contentment or once again give undue room for discontentment?

In your second time around would you allow divine love to surround you. Would you permit ungodliness persistently or embrace unrighteousness insistently? Would you be perceived better-off or would you be presumed worse-off?

Unending Toiling

Endless nights you have experienced unending days so prolonged you have witnessed.

All things in your life seems to ameltorate and amalgamates.

You are at a crossroad.

You are under intense crossfire.

Time usually accelerates.

Time never decelerates.

Your life is on the down-turn.

Your life is going down the drain.

My Lord Jesus-Christ uttered, I will never desert you.

My savior muttered, he will never ever decline you.

Give me the totality of your heart.

Your burden is eased, all your fears will depart.

All your sorrows in the coming days.

My grace is sufficient to weather successfully the stormy days.

My counsel is, repose trust in me.

You will not be misled.

You will not be misguided.

The Siege

The dark clouds gathered momentum, lightning intensifies it's action artly.

A storm was approaching. I had an overview of it's imminent surfacing.

Quietly and dutifully I watched this intruder repugnantly.

My mood put mildly, to say the least was hostile.

The flashlights was deletertous.

The rumblings was devastating.

The wind was intensely destructive.

There was a creation of the atmosphere of foreboding.

My life was imploding in practical terms, everything was eroding. Effortlessly I started brooding about the way and manner this menacing outbreak terminated.

At the zenith and apex of the assault I was visibly and noticeably fretful.

I was frozen with fear during the darkest, gloomiest and bleakest days ahead lies a better and promising days.

God's intervention is secured.

His leading is superb.

His guidance and direction is supreme.

The possibility of problems remains.

The inevitability of siege could not be resisted. Fear of the unknown have been relegated by the all-knowing God.

Firmly and tenaciously I am holding on to the love that is unfolding via his grace I can aptly and accurately predicts the ending.

I am perpetually and everlastingly safe and secured in his unseen and invisible hands.

Vacating Depression

1.   You have dwelt too extensively in the abyss of depression.

You have overspent your time in the solitary confinement of abyssmal oblivion.

It is time to retrace your steps.

It is time to reconsider your ways.

How far have you withdrawn.

How far have you vehemently withstand.

You can repunge.

You can resist.

You have grown too recluse.

Your thoughts have crashed.

Your emotions are crushed.

Stop the hasping.

and the clasping.

Your life is redundant.

You are increasingly retrogressing.

2.   Leave the shell of recluse.

Crawl out of the domain of disuse.

Never consider yourself of no earthly good.

Do not neglect what you should.

Your dreams are indisputably shattered

They have turned to ashes and dust.

There are still an array of individuals meriting or worthy of trust.

Forget about the gloominess and bleakness.

Incontestably life is unjust.

Forget about the loneliness you can adjust.

Give Him Grace

May he face life's problems and challenges as he faced his broken bike when he was small, working till he traced and located each problem to its source and fixed it all. This was a challenge he had accept with curiosity. He worked night and day. What is loosing sleep when interest is involved? Hobby or problem he never relent in its efforts or turned it loose till it was successfully tackled and solved. Now he is a man and man-sized problems stare him in the face. Interested or not Lord, grant him grace as this is a problem tough, and not a toy, so too he is a man, Lord not a boy anymore. Yet in the boy he once was I could clearly, vividly and unobtrusively see delightful glimpses of the man he would eventually becomes. I could equally accurately projected the kind of father he would later in life become in the light of the caring attitude he has exhibited over the years. I can predict with a pinpoint accuracy the type of husband he most indisputably will turned out to be. I could unarguably rightly conclude the kind of profession or vocation he would dabble into taking into cognizance or consideration his keen interest in studying the Bible and his constant involvement in the things that possesses spiritual or eternal value or significance.

Poem on Relentless Yearning (12/12/08)

If I lived within the sound
of the sea's relentless yearning,
my soul would rise and fly to seek
what the soul longs for unable to speak
aware as I go, of him everywhere.
In my heart, in the clouds, in the cold wet
air.
And my soul would worship in joyful prayer
receeding as the waves recede.
Returning with the waves returning,
Reaching up as for him, feeling.
When with the waves kneeling
Kneeling.
Kneeling in reverential kneeling.

Kneeling in adoration, kneeling to praise

The only gloriously glorious, perfectly

perfect, lovingly loving, mercifully merciful, sovereignly God. Faithfully-faithful infallibly infallible. God I earnestly yearn to be in your abiding presence, longing for your invigorating and refreshing power, ardently looking forward with unparallel anticipation a rush, the intolerable craving for your blissful fellowship shievers throughout like a trumpet call – and I unhesitatingly and ecstaticly embrace your unending and enduring love and war

THE BRIGHT SIDE OF FAILURE

Just as Brother John of old prepares the way for our Creator, Lord and God Jesus Christ, so also failure prepares the way for success. So brothers and sisters, when you colossally fail in life, try, try, and try again.

Just as our mediator Jesus Christ is the only way, ticket, and passport to heaven, so also is failure a guarantor to success. So brethren try, try, and try again when next failure strikes.

Just as the Bible is crucial to the Christians spiritual growth and development, so also is failure vitally important for success, children of the living God, next time you fail try, try and try again.

As cable wires is essential for jump starting a malfunctioning vehicle, failure jump starts success. Therefore when failure rears it's ugly head-all you need do is try, try and try again.

As the word of God is clearly and indisputably the harbinger of good news, failure unarguably heralds success. Friends, when next failure looms, attack it head on with a renewed vigor. A success equation is considered incomplete without the presence of failure. Suffice to say we must not throw in the towel, but rather persistently pursue success through the means of failure.

Just as honor is the seed for longevity, so also failure is a catalyst for success. Fellow brothers and sisters in Christ, try, try and try again.

Failure is the factory for, and a road map for success, children of the most high God, if you miss it once, retrace your steps and try, try, and try again.

Success is failure turned inside out. The silver tint of the clouds of doubt and you never can tell how noticeably and significantly close you are. It may be near when it seems to far.

DO NOT QUIT

When things go wrong as they
Sometimes will,
When the road you are traveling
Seems all up hill,
When the food is low and the debts are
High,
And you want to smile, but you have
To sigh,
When care is pressing you down a bit,
Rest if you must, but don't you quit.
Life is queer with it's twists and turns,
As every one of us sometimes learns.
And many a failure turns about,
When he might have won.

Gallant Departure

The universe is a stage.

Every individual is an actor and actress we are all destined by our maker (God) to play our part in the mammoth drama called the earth just as actors and actress are allocated a role, a function in the secular world; the bunch of them coming together produces an interesting and entertaining drama playing a role in the drama of life is crucial. Playing the role successfully is not of vital importance. Actors and actresses are men and women, mortal beings with a knack, flair and propensity to unhibitedly portray life's joys and sorrow on the stage whether we are Thespians (these are professional actors and a actresses) in the traditional sense or not, we are all playing. A prominent role in God's timeless redemptive drama of the ages. All the world is a stage, the greatest poet of all time (William Shakespeare) declared the most respected voice in literature was indeed right to a considerable extent. The best performers knew how to most gracefully exit the stage after a terrific and hilarious joke, a beautiful song, an amazing dance, or an astounding display of skill. An actor and actress that is worthy of his or her vocation and indeed something to write home about pull the crowd along and always leave the audience screaming, begging and craving wanting for more. Sadly and unfortunately enough we do not always make as graceful an ?????????????? we would like. Knowing how and when to make a graceful exit necessitates some measure of wisdom on our part as actors and actresses in God's drama. Interestingly, in life, most exits are marked with four red capital letters. Exit. In the spiritual realm reverse is always the case. To say the least is distinctly different. More often than not our exit from difficult situations usually culminates and ended up awkwardly, to put it mildly and kindly suffice to say we need God's wisdom and unlimited grace to know how to detach ourselves from all possible entanglements of this world so as to receive God's help as he speaks to us from the wings during the tumultuous and dire moments when we need him most. Helpful insights possesses the actors and actresses in the drama of life. The director general of the drama of life (God) thoroughly and extensively prepares his children (you and I) to effectively departs this world leaving our marks upon the sand of time as a legacy. Sadly, making a graceful exit in life is sometimes unattainable. There is a damaged relationship left unattended, life encumbrances and entanglements with the world and its temptations, a colossal failure, negligence in personal responsibility, and a period characterized and marked with inactivities We feel like we are a contestant on life's gong show; like we slipped and fell on America's Got Talent or we have just been jeered at, scorn at, uttered a derisive and derogatory remarks to by the viewing audience or were just booed on to the street by the Apollo crowd.

POEM ON FEAR

The arch enemy of mankind. The unrepentant equal destroyer. You are not a respecter of persons by any stretch or imagination. You have a proven track record of equal destruction. Both blacks and white, young and old, rich and poor, great and small have suffered from your unrelentlessness. You have griped many hearts and cut them into shreds. You have attacked innumerable homes and consequently permanently ruined them. You have plagued countless marriages and eventually crumbled them. You have besieged uncountable churches and successfully rendered them unfocused on their lord and master Jesus Christ. You have tampered with the destinies of the multitudes of people and strictly circumvent their fulfillment. You have unregrettably dash the hope of legions of people. You have sabotaged the dreams of sea of people and thus perpetually paralyzed them. You are a very potent, effective and efficient weapon of your master and manufacturer – Satan. You unmistakably and glaringly shares the three fold ministry of your superior – Satan. You are globally prevalent. You are characteristically domineering and indomitable. You are invincible to those outside Jesus Christ my savior and redeemer. Glory be to God the Father, God the Son and God the Holy Spirit you are already gallantly defeated by our sovereign messiah over two thousand years ago. You are notorious for scattering, you have never once gathered if left unchecked and uncurbed you can reduce the entire world into a single continent a continent into a country, a country into a state, a state into a city or town, a city into a village, a village into a hamlet, a hamlet into a hut. You are potentially dangerous to all Christians without exception. You produces in us lack of faith in God. You are popularly known for claiming precious lives before the cold hand of death snatches them. You are a terror of great repute and any life visited by you is marked with helplessness. You have unobtrusively captivated the minds of army or sea of humanities. You have wrecked havoc and pain in the lives of masses of people. You have done bespeakable and dastardly acts in the lives of your unfortunate victims. You have side-tracked the productivity and usefulness of many lives. You have symphoned lives out of the host of people. You have thwarted the avalanche of efforts of progressive minded people. You have foiled noble and meticulous plans of countless people. You are a cruel taskmaster who daily enslaves and delights in tyranizing the weak. You have kept numerous lives in constant bondage. You have undoubtedly dashed the hopes of the hopefuls. You have indisputably hanged the hopes of too many people in the balance. A lot of dreams remain largely unrealized courtesy of your infiltration. You are as ruthless and brutal as your master – Satan. You have permeated and eaten deep into the very fabric of the modern society and world. You have made life more elusive for many souls. You have saddened and make many hearts skipped and throbbed.

Helplessness. Cowardice is one of your closest ally. Worry and anxiety are your prominent and principal helpmate. Villain, beniignant, vicious are the words that aptly, rightly and accurately describes you. When you have an in road in an individuals life, you will create there in a future fright put differently fear of the future.

JESUS, THE ONLY APPROACHABLE GOD.

There are as many Gods and goddesses as there are people on the surface of the earth. How many of them have all their five senses. How many of them can sincerely talk, smell, see, hear, feel or perceive. Many are that conspicuously lacks all the aforementioned characteristics. Without mincing words and incontestably with out an aiota of doubt none except Jesus Christ the God of the Bible, none, none, none except the God revealed in Jesus Christ of Nazareth is indeed approachable. People of this modern day and time ought not to succumb too low, to be gullible enough as to worship and serve a god who cannot feel what they feel, neither relate with them on a one on one or personal basis. It is almost incredulous but true that people, despite advancement in technology civilization, scientific discoveries and invention are still dogmatic enough condescending to a position of dogmatism religiously speaking, embracing a religion whose founder was as helpless in any given situation as themselves. Traveling from continent to continent far and wide, all in a desperate bid or quest to search and seek for any god that is approachable beside the Holy God portrayed in the Bible. Alas I cannot find any unrelenting I was in my goal and pursuit. All these are to no avail. Relating with all manners of people from all walks of life, interacting and mingling with all people of various political religious, social, economic and educational back grounds. All these amounts to vain! Vain! Vain! Searching for an approachable God other than Jesus Christ most unarguably will always amount to a sheer waste of time. Searching for such from one end of the earth to another is a misdirected effort for none actually exist that passes the test of approachability. Fruitlessly, ceaselessly I searched endlessly courtesy of adventure and curiosity and in the names and sakes of these vital human endeavor. Driven, goaded and propelled I was to satisfy my one man search and hunt for a life time goal and ambition. Jesus Christ passed the test of approachability because he is not seated in heaven, looking down through the sky disapprovingly at the world he created. He is not a super-sized or supreme being who care less about starving babies all around the world. He rightly demonstrated this during his earthly ministerial assignment. Sharply rebuked he, his disciples when they were about disuading children to come on to him. In all sincerity, Jesus frowns at every manner and manifestation of slavery, sex slavery, inclusive. Everyone detests and loathes serving an angry God. The God revealed in Jesus Christ as rightly presented in the gospel is not an angry God. By all accounts and estimation, he is a cheerful and happy God. By the way what is the identity and nature of the God of the universe. He was not immuned from suffering when he lived with us. He suffered rejection of various degree from time to time. Humiliation was part and parcel of his thirty three years of existence on earth. What about excruciating physical pain, oh yes, lots and lots of it he experienced. Betrayed he was by his most intimate and closest friend just like you and me. Equally as highly approachable God, Jesus Christ suffered the pangs of death. Friends what is the prerequisite for approaching this magnificently attentive God. Eschew all display of intimidation and fright. Emotion of fear is not uncommon when it comes to world religion. Burning bush experience of Moses is a testament to this. Kneeling and touching the ground five times a day as it is the case in Islam bear witness to the aforementioned offering Hindu sacrifices in the temple is an eye opener, an indicator and pointer to the above mentioned fact. Friends do not be deceived by pluralism of religion. There was, there is currently, and there will be just one and only approachable God Jesus Christ from eternity to eternity, from everlasting to everlasting, from generation to generation. Is there any being more approachable than a baby who is found lying in a manger on Christmas morning.

His demands are not cumbersome
For we all know he is very wholesome
His laws are not grievious
Strictly forbidden is grief
As it is very detestable determination
To be in his plan, requires determination
If sincerity is shown no deterioration
Is expressed and expected
Of every creature of his, high is his expectation
Since his interest is keen and extreme
A sovereign God who is above
Ceaselessly and generously doles out love
The love the displayed and dispensed
Has a more attractive and alluring
Fragrant and aroma than all the lavenders
In the world combined
There is no match for this combination
Realization of heavenly mandate requires no possession of mansion
Undoubtedly every man is simply a speck
In the mighty ocean of earth.
No allocation is ascribe to speculation
But there is a place for specialties

Needless to say that ultimately

Success in life involves no ultimatum

But walking cooperatively with our maker

Since none can achieve a meaningful

Life outside the only true God

Who in comparison is infinitely stronger than all gods.

POEM ON HOPE

You are a virtue divinely given by God. You belong to the future. You are the spiritual eye that distinctly peer and see the overview of the nearest and distant future. You stretch out your hands in the darkest moment beckoning and beseeching whoever will to join his or her hands with yours so as to see the light at the end of the tunnel, twist, turn and bends of life. You thrust out your hands to accompany the individuals who will deem it necessary to look and rise above the visible to behold the unseen transcends the visible to embrace the invisible. You are a medicine to the heart in the same way and manner music is food to the soul. You always see eye to eye with the most high God on every matter. You are the discerner and navigator of tomorrow. You are of the most potent and powerful tool in the hands of the infinitely gracious God. To obtain and secure the future you collide with insurmountable mountains and crumble it in pieces. You attach the impossibilities and scatter it. You emerge victorious over all challenges that dare and stands in your way. You and the spirit of man plays a somewhat similar role in the life of mortal beings. While doubt and flesh are birds of the same feather flocking together. You war relentlessly and unabatedly against doubt and you always come out gallantly and triumphantly. You regularly defeats doubt hands down. You are the anchorage for uncertainties. You are the guiding light to the unknown. You are the intimate ally of faith. You are a solace to the discouraged and weary hearts. Despondence and despair evaporate into thin air. Both gloomness and bleakness. You are the proverbial clock of fortune that dispenses goodness and favor to whoever will patiently wait for you. You are joy and delight to behold in tumultuous and distressing austere economic crisis and time.

Who else?

Who else was born of a virgin Which was prophesied of old? Who else walked to
Calvary To save your Soul?

Who else fed five thousand people, With two fish and five loaves of bread? Who else was
crucified And then rose from the dead?

Who else was sinless And nailed to a cross? Who else took all your sins, That your soul
would not be lost?

Who else raised a dead man Four days dead in the tomb? Who else Gives us Joy and
takes away our gloom?

Who else is so wonderful They call Him The Prince of Peace? Who else do the winds
obey And when He Speaks – they cease?

Who else healed the sick And made the blind to see? Who else Loved enough To die for
you and me?

Who else walked on water And calmed the raging sea? Who else shed His sinless Blood
To set our spirits free?

Who else will be there for you When another friend you cannot find? Who else is so
Forgiving And who else is so Merciful and Kind?

Who else will hug you With compassion in His Eyes? Who else hears your prayers When
you have trouble and you cry?

Who else forgives your sin And still loves you everyday? Who else leads you to Heaven
Like a lamb that went astray?

Who else picks you up With arms gentle and strong? Who else cares enough for you To forgive you from all wrong?

No one else will ever love you like Jesus, No one else can save your soul.

No one else is patiently waiting, to bring you home, No one else is waiting but Jesus.... Jesus Alone.

So come I, Lord! To show my love to Thee;

Yet, like a warrior bold with high elation,

Rush I to combats in my blest vocation. Thy Heart is Guardian of our innocence;

Not once shall it deceive my confidence

Wholly my hopes are placed in Thee, dear Lord!

After long exile, I Thy Face adored

In heaven shall see. When clouds the skies overcast.

To Thee, my Jesus! I lift up my head;

For, in Thy tender glance, these words I see:

"O child! I made My radiant heaven for thee." I know it well – my burning tears and sighs

Are full of charm for Thy benignant eyes.

Strong seraphs form in heaven Thy court divine,

Yet Thou dost seek this poor weak heart of mine.

Ah! take my heart! Jesus, 'tis Thee alone;

All my desires I yield to Thee, my Own!

And all my friends, that are so loved by me,

No longer will I love them, save in Thee!

Appreciation of Jesus's worthiness. Appreciation of all He had done for us.

Jesus Only

Oh, how my heart would spent itself, to bless;

It hath such need to prove its tenderness!

And yet what heart can my heart comprehend?

What heart shall always love me without end?

All – all in vain for such return seek I;

Jesus alone my soul can satisfy.

Naught else contents or charms me here below;

Created things no lasting joy bestow.
My peace, my joy, my love, O Christ!

Thou alone! Thou hast sufficed.
Thou didst know how to make a mother's heart;

Most-tender of fathers, Lord! to me Thou art.

My only Love, Jesus, Divine Word!

More than maternal is Thy heart, dear Lord!

Each moment Thou my way dost guard and guide;

I call – at once I find Thee at my side –

And if, sometimes Thou hide Thy face from me,

Thou Thyself to help me seek for Thee.
Thee, Thee, alone I choose: I am Thy bride.

Unto Thy arms I hasten, there to hide.

Thee would I love, as little children love;

For Thee, like warrior bold, my love I'd prove.

He rule and reign there

His dominion extends here

He is the Commander in chief of life here

And the Chief Executive of Life hereafter.

This is why humans must bow to his wish

And gives no consideration

Nor any form of recognition

To any manifestation of wishful thinking.

We stand to gain when and if he is the centre of our